HOW TO
PRONOUNCE
FRENCH
CORRECTLY

D1516440

Stanley W.
Dominique Poiriel

PASSPORT BOOKS
NTC/Contemporary Publishing Group

Library of Congress Cataloging-in-Publication Data
is available from the United States Library of Congress.

NOTE ON RECORDED MATERIAL
All references to recorded material on audiocassette
are equally applicable to the compact disc version of
this program.

Published by Passport Books
A division of NTC/Contemporary Publishing Group, Inc.
4255 West Touhy Avenue, Lincolnwood (Chicago), Illinois 60646-1975 U.S.A.
Copyright © 1990 by NTC/Contemporary Publishing Group, Inc.
Printed in the United States of America
International Standard Book Number: 0-8442-1522-8
9 0 VP 19 18 17 16 15 14 13 12 11 10

Contents

Introduction

How to Pronounce French Correctly is a comprehensive, self-contained program that will enable you to quickly master the pronunciation of French, including vowels, consonants, linking, elision, and intonation patterns.

This unique program is designed for students in

- introductory French classes who need a brief, efficient introduction to the sound system of the language
- intermediate and advanced classes who require a short but comprehensive review of the sound patterns of French to improve their pronunciation
- self-study programs at any level, where materials must be presented with exceptional clarity

Consisting of this Study Guide and a convenient audiocassette, *How to Pronounce French Correctly* covers all significant aspects of French pronunciation. The contents of the Study Guide and audiocassette have been organized logically and in keeping with sound methodological principles: First you will master the five simple vowels of French; then the nasal vowel sounds and the vowel combinations; next, the consonants, presented in order from easiest to most challenging; following these are practical exercises on consonant combinations, linking, and elision; and finally, the unit on intonation presents the pitch patterns of French in sentences that draw together all the pronunciation features taught in the program.

A very straightforward, uncomplicated approach to this program is to simply play the audiocassette, reading silently as you listen to the descriptions of the sounds; then, still following along in the Study Guide, repeat the words, phrases, and sentences modeled by the native speaker. Rewind the cassette as many times as necessary to learn the materials, and fully master each lesson before going on to the next. Review at regular intervals. The design of the program also permits use of the audiocassette without this Study Guide in circumstances where you can listen but not read—as when driving an automobile. For most students, twenty to thirty minutes is an optimal time period for efficient study. After you have learned to associate the sounds with the letters of the French alphabet, you will be able to continue practicing with the cassette without the Study Guide.

Learning to pronounce the sounds of another language involves both mental and physical effort. Mentally, you must learn to associate sounds with symbols—in this case, letters of the French alphabet with the sounds they represent. Physically, you must master sounds that often do not exist in English—a task that resembles learning the "fundamentals" of a sport, because it involves coordination and muscular skills. Many of the sound patterns of French closely resemble those of English and will be easy for you to learn and remember; others contrast strongly, and mastering them will require special effort; all can be pronounced accurately by virtually any student willing to devote the time and energy needed to form good speech habits.

A key concept in preparing this program has been to keep it simple, practical, and *nontechnical.* In describing sounds, the jargon of descriptive linguistics has generally been avoided, and where linguistic terms are used they are always defined in the text; while individuals with strong backgrounds in articulatory phonetics may miss the technical terms, most students will appreciate the fact that *How to Pronounce French Correctly* does not submit them to excessively detailed linguistic descriptions better suited to a descriptive grammar than to a program designed for classroom practice. Decades of classroom experience have shown the authors that students cannot master the intonation patterns of French by reading complicated linguistic descriptions of them; in fact, such descriptions tend to discourage most learners. *How to Pronounce French Correctly* presents the key intonation patterns of French simply, without the confusion of musical notes, numbers, wriggly curves, and angular lines that clutter many texts.

The vocabulary used in the examples is limited to everyday words and avoids the obscure lexical items that some authors utilize to create "minimal pair" drills.

Like other languages, French has many dialects, both regional and social. The dialect presented in this program—generally referred to as *International French*—represents the pronunciation of cultured native Parisians. It is the French heard in the media and taught in FFL classrooms throughout the world.

We hope that this brief work will ease the task of students learning the sound patterns of French, and of teachers striving to present them clearly. These materials are designed to meet the need for a comprehensive and sufficiently but not excessively detailed program for introducing and reviewing the sounds of French.

A final word as you study the details of French pronunciation in words, phrases, and brief sentences: Never lose sight of the reality that each word you utter bears a fragment of the culture of a great people; through your efforts you can achieve the ultimate purpose of second-language study—understanding across cultures.

Part One
French Letters and Sounds

Unit 1

The Vowels a, e, i, o, and u

French has only five vowel letters, but each represents more than one sound. To master these sounds you must first be able to hear and distinguish them, then produce them. As you listen and repeat the French vowels, notice how each is pronounced clearly and energetically.

The Letter a

The letter **a** has two pronunciations. The first and most common is a sound between the *a* of *father* and the *a* in *cat*.

	EXAMPLES	MEANING
Say:	**ma**	my
	madame	Mrs., madam
	chat	cat
	facile	easy
	montagne	mountain
	capitale	capital (city)

The other pronunciation of the French letter **a**—sometimes called **open a**—sounds much like the *a* in English *father*. It generally occurs before **ss** or before final **s,** or is written as a circumflex **â.***

---

* The distinction between these two **a** sounds is being less and less observed; it now occurs mainly in a few near-homonyms such as:

        pâte (dough, batter)   **patte** (paw, foot, leg)
        mâle (male)   **mal** (pain, harm)

1

Say:	**basse**	low (f. adj.)
	passe	pass (noun)
	bas	low (m. adj.)
	pas	step
	âge	age
	château	chateau, castle

The Letter e

This letter has three pronunciations, and is also sometimes silent:

1. Often, it sounds like the *a* in English *late* /leYt/, but without the "off-glide" (represented here as /Y/). This **closed e** sound occurs when the letter **e**

bears an acute accent (**é**):

Say:	**café**	coffee, café
	difficulté	difficulty
	bébé	baby
	répété	repeated

occurs as word-final **-er, -ed, -ez**:

Say:	**trouver**	to find
	pied	foot
	allez	you go

occurs in one-syllable words ending in **-es**:*

Say:	**les**	the, them
	des	of the, some
	mes	my
	tes	your

---

* Actually, the words in this particular category do not have a set pronunciation; they may be pronounced with a **closed e** or with an **open e** as in English *let*.

2. The second pronunciation of the French letter **e** sounds like the *e* in English *let.* This *e,* called the **open e,** occurs when this letter

bears a grave accent (**è**):

Say:	**près**	near
	très	very
	nièce	niece
	quatrième	fourth

bears a circumflex accent (**ê**):

Say:	**prêt**	ready
	rêve	dream
	tête	head
	forêt	forest

or occurs in a syllable ending in a pronounced consonant:

Say:	**avec**	(a-vec)	with
	espagnol	(es-pa-gnol)	Spanish
	excellent	(ex-cel-lent)	excellent
	correct	(cor-rect)	correct

3. The third pronunication of the French **e** is called **mute e,** and resembles the *e* of English *the.* It occurs

in one-syllable words ending in **e:**

Say:	**le**	the, him, it
	me	me, to me
	te	you, to you
	se	himself, herself

and at the end of syllables that are not word-final:

Say:	**devoir**	(de-voir)	should, must
	petit	(pe-tit)	small
	relever	(re-le-ver)	to raise again
	avenue	(a-ve-nue)	avenue

4. Finally, the **silent** or **unpronounced e** occurs

as unaccented **e** at the end of words of more than one syllable:

Say:

facile	easy
quelle	which, what
capitale	capital (city)

when the last syllable ends in **-es** with the **s** forming the plural, or in the third person plural present verb ending **-ent:**

Say:

faciles	easy
quelles	which, what
capitales	capitals (cities)
trouvent	they find

when, in a syllable other than the first, the letter **e** follows a single consonant sound and is the final letter in the syllable:

Say:

finalement	finally
appeler	to call
acheter	to buy
élevé	high

The Letter i

This letter has basically the sound of the vowel in English *see* /seeY/, but without the off-glide (shown here as /Y/).

Say:

difficile	difficult
limite	limit
il	he
île	island
machine	machine
ici	here

Occasionally and mainly in proper nouns, this same sound is represented by the letter **y:**

Say:		
	Yves	(man's name)
	Ypres	(city in Belgium)
	Nancy	(city in France)

When the French letter **i** is followed by another pronounced vowel, it is pronounced like the *y* of English *yes.*

Say:		
	officiel	official
	supérieur	superior
	société	society
	spécial	special
	viande	meat

The Letter o

The most common pronunciation of the French letter **o** is called the **open o;** it resembles the vowel of English *bought,* and usually occurs in a syllable ending in a consonant.

Say:		
	porte	door
	mort	dead
	poste	post office
	alors	then
	bonne	good
	porc	pork

The other pronunciation of the letter **o** is called the **closed o.** Pronounce it like the *o* of English *no* / noW /, but without the off-glide (shown here as / W /)

when it is written as circumflex **ô:**

Say:		
	côte	coast, hill
	bientôt	soon
	nôtre	ours
	rôle	role

diplôme	diploma
plutôt	rather

when it precedes a **z** sound:

Say:	**imposer**	to impose
	rose	rose
	position	position
	poser	to put
	chose	thing
	oser	to dare

or when it is the last sound in a word (Final **t** and **s** in the following words are silent.):

Say:	**mot**	word
	stylo	pen
	vos	your
	gros	large
	dos	back
	piano	piano

The Letter u

The French letter **u** has no English equivalent. To pronounce it, round your lips as if to pronounce the *oo* of English *cool;* then, holding them in that position, pronounce the *ee* of *need.*

Say:	**lune**	moon
	une	a, an, one (f.)
	plus	more, most
	sur	on, over
	sûr	sure
	naturel	natural

Note: French Accent Marks

There are three written accents used with French vowels:

(´) the **acute accent,** used only over **e**
(`) the **grave accent,** used over **a, e,** and **u**
(^) the **circumflex accent,** used over **a, e, i, o,** and **u**

These accent marks have three uses:

First, they indicate how to pronounce the vowel:

â	= **open a**	**âge**	**château**
è or **ê**	= **open e**	**près**	**très**
é	= **closed e**	**café**	**bébé**
ô	= **closed o**	**rôle**	**diplôme**

Second, they distinguish *homonyms* (words spelled alike but having different meanings):

a	has	**à**	to
la	the	**là**	there
ou	or	**où**	where
sur	on	**sûr**	sure

Third, they show that, over time, a word has lost an **s:**

côte	coast
forêt	forest
hôpital	hospital

Unit 2_____

The Nasal Vowel Sounds

To pronounce nasal vowel sounds, pass part of the sound through the nose—rather than all through the mouth as you do with English vowels, which are nonnasal.

French nasal vowel sounds occur when any vowel letter is followed by **m** or **n** in the same syllable. French has four nasal vowel sounds, each with several spellings:

1. The first sounds like the *a* in English *father,* but with some of the air passing through the nose:

SPELLING		EXAMPLES	MEANING
am	Say:	**ample**	ample
		ambassadeur	ambassador
an		**an**	year
		anglais	English
em		**temps**	time
		emporter	to carry off
en		**en**	in
		dent	tooth

2. The second is like the vowel in English *let,* but again diverting some air through the nose:

SPELLING		EXAMPLES	MEANING
im	Say:	**impossible**	impossible
		simple	simple
in		**fin**	end
		intérieur	interior

aim	**faim**	hunger
ain	**main**	hand
	pain	bread
ein	**plein**	full
	peintre	painter
en	**examen**	examination
(i)e	**citoyen**	citizen
	bien	well
	rien	nothing

3. The third resembles the vowel in English *ought,* but allowing some of the air to pass through the nose:

SPELLING		EXAMPLES	MEANING
om	Say:	**nombre**	number
		compter	to count
on		**mon**	my
		question	question

4. And the fourth is like the vowel in English *learn,* again allowing some air to pass through the nose:*

SPELLING		EXAMPLES	MEANING
um	Say:	**humble**	humble
		parfum	perfume
un		**un**	one
		lundi	Monday

---

* Note, however, that this nasal vowel sound is now often pronounced like the nasal vowel of **fin,** *end.*

Notes on French Syllabification

In order to pronounce some French sounds correctly—such as the nasal vowels before **m** and **n**—it is convenient to know how to divide French words into syllables. This is quite easy: There are four simple rules.

1. A single consonant always goes with the following vowel:

a-mi	friend
a-ni-mal	animal
cra-va-te	tie
ca-pi-ta-le	capital
ma-da-me	Mrs., madam
té-lé-vi-sion	television

2. Two consonants within a word are generally divided.

men-tir	to lie
im-por-tant	important
mon-sieur	Mr., sir
par-le	he / she speaks
par-tie	part, game
pas-ser	to spend, to pass

continued

3. The combination of consonant plus **l** or **r** goes with the following vowel:

bl	**pro-blè-me**	problem
br	**cé-lè-bre**	famous
cl	**ac-cla-mer**	to cheer
cr	**dé-cret**	decree
dr	**ci-dre**	cider
fl	**in-fla-tion**	inflation
fr	**a-fri-cain**	African
gl	**rè-gle**	rule
gr	**pro-grès**	progress
pl	**a-pla-nir**	to level
pr	**a-près**	after
tr	**pa-trie**	native land
vr	**ou-vri-er**	worker

4. The following consonant combinations, pronounced as single sounds, go with the following vowel:

ch	**a-che-ter**	to buy
gn	**mon-ta-gne**	mountain
ill	**tra-va-iller**	to work
ph	**té-lé-pho-ne**	telephone
th	**ca-thé-dra-le**	cathedral

Unit 3 _____

Vowel Combinations

French words feature a number of vowel combinations. Most of them are pronounced as simple vowels. Practice the following key words for the French vowel combinations.

ai

This combination has two pronunciations. Most often it is pronounced as **open e,** that is, like the vowel sound in English *let.*

Say:	**air**	air
	lait	milk
	mais	but
	raison	reason
	semaine	week

The second pronunciation of **ai** is like **closed e** (the vowel sound in English *late,* but without the "off-glide"). It occurs when **ai** is the final sound of a verb ending.

Say:	**je parlerai**	I will talk
	je finirai	I will finish
	je viendrai	I will come
	je dormirai	I will sleep
	je mangerai	I will eat
	je donnerai	I will give

au, eau

These two vowel combinations are usually pronounced like **closed o,** the vowel in English *no,* but without the off-glide.

Say:	**au**	to the
	gauche	left

automne	autumn
eau	water
bateau	boat
couteau	knife

ei

Pronounce this vowel combination like the **open e** of English *let.*

Say:	**peine**	trouble, pain
	reine	queen
	neige	snow
	seize	sixteen
	seigneur	lord
	veine	vein

eu, œu

These vowel combinations have no equivalent in English, but are easy to master because they consist of elements you already know. There are two pronunciations, **open** and **closed.**

 The **open** version is much like the **open e** of English *let,* but with the lips rounded. It occurs in syllables ending in a consonant.

Say:	**peur**	fear
	seul	only, alone
	heure	hour
	erreur	error
	bœuf	ox, steer
	cœur	heart
	œuf	egg
	sœur	sister

Pronounce the closed version like a **closed e**—the vowel in English *late*—but without the off-glide, and with your lips rounded. This sound occurs when this vowel combination is the last sound in a word or syllable . . .

Say:	**peu**	not much, not many
	bleu	blue
	nerveux	nervous
	heureux	happy
	adieu	goodbye
	sérieux	serious
	vœu	wish, vow

. . . or before a final **z** sound (the letter **s** between vowels).

Say:	**creuse**	empty, hollow
	heureuse	happy
	nerveuse	nervous
	nombreuse	numerous
	sérieuse	serious

oi

Pronounce this vowel combination somewhat like the *wa* of English *water*.

Say:	**moi**	me
	roi	king
	fois	time
	voilà	there is, there are
	étoile	star
	histoire	story

ou

This French vowel combination has two pronunciations. Usually it sounds like the *ou* in English *group,* but without the off-glide.

Say:	**ou**	or
	sous	under
	cousin	cousin

amour	love
fou	crazy
jour	day

But when another pronounced vowel follows it, **ou** has the sound of *w* in English *west*.

Say:	**oui**	yes
	ouest	west
	Louis	Louis
	Édouard	Edward

ui

Pronounce this vowel combination as follows:

1. With your lips rounded, pronounce the *ee* of English *see,* but rapidly and without the off-glide.
2. Follow it with French **i,** which is like the *ee* of English *see,* but without lip rounding.

Say:	**huit**	eight
	lui	to him / her
	je suis	I am
	suisse	Swiss
	suivant	following
	tout de suite	immediately

Unit 4_____

The Consonants **f, h, s,** and **w**

The French Consonants: General Notes

1. Generally, written consonants at the end of French words are silent:

Examples:		
	français	French
	trop	too many, too much
	départ	departure
	livres	books
	nom	name
	nord	north

But final **c, r, f,** and **l**—the consonants of **CaReFuL**—are usually pronounced.

Examples:		
	parc	park
	fier	proud
	neuf	nine
	mal	pain, trouble, evil

2. The French letters **b, d, k, m, n, v,** and **z** are pronounced so much like their English counterparts that specific exercises are not needed for their mastery.

The Letter f

Unlike most other French consonants, the **f** is usually pronounced when it is word-final.

Say:		
	bœuf	ox, steer
	chef	chief, head
	neuf	nine
	œuf	egg
	soif	thirst

Sometimes the **f** sound is written as **ph:**

Say:		
	photo	photo
	photocopie	photocopy
	pharmacie	pharmacy, drugstore
	philosophie	philosophy
	phrase	sentence

The Letter h

Like the *h* of English *honor,* French **h** is always silent. Each of the following words begins with silent **h:**

Say:		
	haut	high
	héros	hero
	heure	hour, time
	homme	man
	hier	yesterday
	hôpital	hospital

The Letter s

Like the English *s,* this French letter has two sounds: When it is initial, when it occurs between a vowel and a consonant, or when written as **ss,** pronounce it like the *s* of English *see.*

Say:		
	sa	his, her, its
	soleil	sun
	système	system

suspect	suspect
classe	class
impossible	impossible

But when it occurs alone between two vowels, pronounce the French **s** like the *z* in English *zoo.*

Say:	**rose**	rose
	chose	thing
	occasion	occasion
	magasin	store
	maison	house
	française	French girl, French woman

The Letter w

This letter occurs in *loan words,* that is, words brought into French from other languages. It is generally pronounced like the *v* of English *very,* or sometimes as an English *w.*

Say:	**wagon**	(v)	truck, wagon
	watt	(w)	watt
	week-end	(w)	weekend
	Washington	(w)	Washington
	whisky	(w)	whiskey

The Consonants p, t, c, and q

The Letter p

The pronunciation of this French letter is like that of English *p*, but without *aspiration* (the slight puff of air heard in the letter *p* of English *part*).

Say:
papa	dad
poire	pear
pipe	pipe
populaire	popular
public	public
penser	to think

The Letter t

French **t** has two sounds. The first is like English *t*, but again, avoid the aspiration as heard in the *t* of English *table*.

Say:
table	table
temps	time
timbre	stamp
tout	all
tu	you

The second pronunciation of **t** is like the *s* of English *see*. Use it in words ending in

-tion	Say:	**action**	action
		nation	nation
-tial		**partial**	partial (biased)
		initial	initial

-tie	**démocratie**	democracy
	aristocratie	aristocracy
-tiel	**potentiel**	potential
	partiel	partial (incomplete)
-tieux	**ambitieux**	ambitious
	superstitieux	superstitious

The Letter c

In the combinations **ca, co,** and **cu,** or when it is the final letter of a word, the French letter **c** is like the *c* of English *cat,* but without the slight aspiration heard in that word.

Say:	**cahier**	notebook
	calme	calm
	comme	like, as
	culture	culture
	curieux	curious
	avec	with
	public	public
	parc	park

However, before **e** or **i,** pronounce **c** as **s.**

Say:	**célèbre**	famous
	cent	one hundred
	certain	certain
	ciel	sky
	cinq	five
	civil	civil

When written with a **cedilla (ç),** the French **c** is also pronounced as **s.**

Say:	**ça**	that
	français	French

garçon	boy, waiter
avançons	let's move forward
reçu	received

The Letter q

This letter almost always occurs in the combination **qu.** Pronounce it as an English *k,* but without aspiration.

Say:		
	quand	when
	question	question
	qui	who(m), that, which
	tragique	tragic
	paquet	package

Unit 6_____

The Consonants g, j, l, r, and x

The Letter g

When it precedes **a, o, u,** or another consonant, pronounce French **g** like the *g* in English *good.*

Say:

garçon	boy
gare	railroad station
golf	golf
gourmet	gourmet
guerre	war
guide	guide
glace	glass, ice cream
grand	great, large

But before **e** or **i,** it is pronounced like the *s* in English *leisure.* Be sure not to say the *g* sound of English *general.*

Say:

général	general
rouge	red
étrange	strange
girafe	giraffe
magie	magic
tragique	tragic

The Letter j

This letter has the same sound as French **g** before **e** or **i,** so pronounce it like the *s* in English *leisure.* Again, be sure not to say the *g* sound of English *general.*

Say:

jamais	ever, never
jambe	leg

joie	joy
joli	pretty
juillet	July
bijou	jewel

The Letter l

French l is quite different from its English counterpart. The tip of your tongue must touch your upper front teeth. Also pronounce it more tensely than the *l* of English *tell*.

Say:	**la**	the, her, it
	langue	language
	lentement	slowly
	facile	easy
	calme	calm
	église	church
	table	table
	simple	simple

You will recall that l is one of the four consonants in the word **CaReFuL,** which are usually pronounced at the ends of words.

Say:	**il**	he, it
	mal	pain, trouble, evil
	quel	which, that
	sel	salt
	hôtel	hotel
	final	final

Double ll is often pronounced like the single l.

Say:	**belle**	beautiful
	mille	thousand
	ville	city, town

bulletin	bulletin
salle	room

But sometimes the **l** or **ll** is pronounced like the *y* in English *yes*. This occurs in the combinations **-ill-,** vowel plus **-ill-,** or vowel plus final **-il.**

Say:	**bri<u>ll</u>ant**	brilliant
	fam<u>ill</u>e	family
	f<u>ill</u>e	daughter, girl
	bat<u>aill</u>e	battle
	bout<u>eill</u>e	bottle
	m<u>eill</u>eur	better
	dé<u>tail</u>	detail
	<u>œil</u>	eye
	sol<u>eil</u>	sun

This same sound is sometimes represented by the letter **y:**

Say:	**voyage**	trip, journey
	payer	to pay
	voyelle	vowel
	yeux	eyes
	yoghurt	yogurt

The Letter r

The Parisian pronunciation of French **r** has been described as sounding "like a gargle." To produce it, place the tip of the tongue against your lower front teeth. Then raise the back of your tongue enough so that the air coming through your throat causes a soft vibrating sound as it passes the **uvula**—that small appendage descending from the soft palate.

Say:	**rouge**	red
	riche	rich
	rôle	role
	route	road, route

bref	short
crayon	pencil
français	French
préférable	preferable
lettre	letter
livre	book

Word-final **r** is pronounced in one-syllable words.

Say:	**air**	air
	car	for, because
	cher	dear
	fer	iron
	jour	day
	soir	evening

But in words of more than one syllable, the final **r** is usually silent.*

Say:	**aller**	to go
	cacher	to hide
	manger	to eat
	étranger	foreign
	millier	thousand
	premier	first

However, there are many exceptions to this. Say these common words of more than one syllable in which final **r** is pronounced:

Say:	**couleur**	color
	hiver	winter
	joueur	player

---

* The final **-r** of the infinitive ending **-er** is always silent, as is the final **r** of words of more than one syllable ending in **-ier**. (Examples: **dernier,** *last;* **familier,** *familiar;* **papier,** *paper,* etc.)

obéir	to obey
supérieur	superior

The Letter x

In **cognates**—French words closely resembling their English counterparts—pronounce French **x** as *ks* or *gz,* as you would in the corresponding English word.

Say:		
	excellence	excellence
	expert	expert
	extravagant	extravagant
	examen	examination
	exemple	example
	existence	existence

Consonant Combinations

Several French consonant combinations—**ch, ph, th, gn,** and **cc**—merit special attention.

ch

Pronounce this combination like the *sh* in English *shine*—never like the *ch* of English *church*.

Say:		
	chacun	each, each one
	cheval	horse
	chose	thing
	chute	fall
	acheter	to buy
	enchanter	to delight, to enchant
	pêcheur	fisherman
	riche	rich

There are a few words in which French **ch** is pronounced like *k* of English *key:*

Say:		
	chrétien*	Christian
	cholestérol	cholesterol
	choral	choral
	chrome	chromium
	chrono(mètre)	stopwatch

---

* When **ch** is followed by **r,** it is always pronounced as *k.*

27

ph

Pronounce this sound like the *ph* in English *photo*.

Say:		
	photo	photo
	phrase	sentence
	orthographe	spelling
	photographie	photography
	philosophie	philosophy
	géographie	geography

th

This combination sounds like the *t* in English *tell*, but without aspiration. Be sure not to pronounce it like the *th* sounds of English *the* or *think*.

Say:		
	thé	tea
	théorie	theory
	thermomètre	thermometer
	théâtre	theater
	cathédrale	cathedral
	méthode	method
	enthousiasme	enthusiasm
	athlétisme	track and field

gn

Although the sound of French **gn** resembles that of the *ny* of English *canyon*, there is a difference. French **gn** is a single consonant sound, while the *ny* of English *canyon* represents two separate sounds, each belonging to a different syllable (*can-yon*).

Say:			
	agneau	(a-gneau)	lamb
	espagnol	(es-pa-gnol)	Spanish
	Espagne		Spain
	champagne		champagne
	ligne		line
	montagne		mountain

signe	sign
signal	signal
gagner	to win, to earn

cc

This combination has two pronunciations. Before **a, o,** or **u,** it sounds like the *k* in English *kitten,* but without aspiration.

Say:	**accabler**	to overwhelm
	accaparer	to monopolize
	acclamer	to cheer
	accompagner	to accompany
	accomplir	to carry out
	accord	agreement
	accuser	to accuse

But before **e** or **i,** pronounce it as **ks.**

Say:	**accent**	accent
	accélérer	to speed up
	accepter	to accept
	accès	access
	accident	accident

Part Two
Special Sound Features

Unit 8

Linking and Elision

These two key features of French must be fully mastered if you wish to speak the language fluently and naturally. Neither is really complicated; by repeating the following examples you can develop the necessary automatic speech habits.

Linking

Linking means the pronunciation of a normally silent word-final consonant before a word that begins with a vowel sound. In spoken French, linking depends on several factors, including

The situation. For example, linking occurs more frequently in a formal speech than in conversation between friends.

The speaker's educational level. Less-educated speakers do less linking.

Whether the speaker is *reading aloud or speaking spontaneously.* "Reading pronunciation" features more linking.

Personal preference. French individualism is reflected in speaking style.

You can understand and master linking by considering the *sounds* and *word types* involved in it.

The Sounds Involved in Linking

In linking, the normally silent final consonants **s, x,** and **z** are all pronounced as **z.**

Say:		
	les‿amis	the friends
	nous‿avons	we have
	ils‿ont	they have
	très‿intéressant	very interesting

aux‿étudiants	to the students
deux‿amis	two friends
dix‿amis	ten friends
six‿heures	six hours
chez‿eux	at their house
Allez‿y.	Go there.
Venez‿ici.	Come here.

Normally silent word-final **d** and **t** are both pronounced as **t**.

Say:

un grand‿ami	a big friend
un grand‿édifice	a big building
quand‿il arrive	when he arrives
quand‿elle retourne	when she returns
un petit‿ami	a little friend
C'est‿ici.	It's here.
Que veut‿il?	What does he want?
mangent‿ils?	do they eat?

Normally silent word-final **n** is pronounced.

Say:

un‿ami	a friend
un‿hôtel	a hotel
un certain‿âge	a certain age
en‿Italie	in Italy
en‿avance	in advance
il y en‿a	there is / there are
un bon‿hôtel	a good hotel

Word-final **f**, **p**, **q**, and **r** are also linked to following vowel sounds.

Say:

neuf‿heures	(f = v)	nine hours
trop‿aimable	(p = p)	too friendly
cinq‿heures	(q = k)	five hours
le premier‿anniversaire	(r = r)	the first anniversary

Word Types and Linking

Four intimate word relationships involve linking; they are

1. Modifier plus noun
2. Subject and verb
3. Preposition and its object, and
4. Adverb and the word it modifies

Let's practice each.

1. Modifier plus Noun

Say:		
	un‿acteur	an actor
	un‿édifice	a building
	les‿automobiles	the automobiles
	les‿amis	the friends
	des‿édifices	some buildings
	des‿amis	some friends
	un petit‿enfant	a small child
	un grand‿enfant	a large child
	beaux‿enfants	beautiful children
	mes‿amis	my friends
	ces‿arbres	these trees
	cet‿étudiant	this student

2. Subject and Verb

Say:		
	nous‿avons	we have
	vous‿êtes	you are
	elles‿arrivent	they arrive
	Où sont‿elles?	Where are they?
	Où est‿il?	Where is he?
	mangent‿ils?	do they eat?

3. Preposition and Its Object

Say:		
	après‿avoir parlé	after having talked
	chez‿elle	at her house

dans_un moment	in a moment
en_avion	by airplane
sans_intérêt	without interest
sous_un_arbre	under a tree

4. Adverb and the Word It Modifies

Say:		
	bien_étrange	very strange
	bien_entendu	of course
	pas_encore	not yet
	pas_un n'est venu	not one came
	plus_intelligent	more intelligent
	de plus_en plus	more and more
	très_intéressant	very interesting
	très_élégant	very elegant

Elision

Elision means dropping the final **e** or **a** of a French word when the following word begins with a vowel sound. In writing, elision is marked by an apostrophe; in speaking, by loss of a vowel sound. In French, you **elide,** or drop vowels, in the following five cases:

1. Drop the final **e** of the one-syllable words **ce, de, je, le, me, ne, que, te,** and **se** before words beginning with a vowel sound.

Say:			
	C'est ici.	(ce̸)	It's here.
	trop d'eau	(de̸)	too much water
	J'ai faim.	(je̸)	I'm hungry.
	Il me donne de l'argent.	(le̸)	He gives me some money.
	Je m'appelle Jean Fortier.	(me̸)	My name is Jean Fortier.
	Ce n'est pas ici.	(ne̸)	It's not here.

Note: Prohibited Linking

Linking *does not* take place
Before a number of words—often of Germanic origin—
that begin with **h:**

> Examples: (* indicates prohibited linking)
> **en * haut**   at the top
> **les * haricots**   the beans
> **deux * héros**   two heroes
> **C'est * honteux!**   It's a disgrace!

After **et** (*and*):

> Examples:
> **Brigitte et * Anne**   Bridget and Ann
> **ma sœur et * un ami**   my sister and a friend

Between a singular noun and following adjective:

> Examples:
> **un soldat * américain**   an American soldier
> **un pantalon * élégant**   elegant trousers

Before **onze, huit,** or **oui:**

> Examples:
> **les * onze enfants**   the eleven children
> **les * huit hommes**   the eight men
> **mais * oui**   (but) of course

Qu'en dites-vous?	(qu¢)	What do you say about it?
Je t'aime.	(t¢)	I like (love) you.
Elle s'appelle Lucie Renoir.	(s¢)	Her name is Lucy Renoir.

2. Drop the final **a** of **la** (*the, her*) before words beginning with a vowel sound.

Say:			
	l'auto	(la̸)	the car
	Je l'aime.	(la̸)	I love her.

l'école	(lₐ)	the school
l'enveloppe	(lₐ)	the envelope
l'idée	(lₐ)	the idea
l'île	(lₐ)	the island
l'omelette	(lₐ)	the omelet
l'université	(lₐ)	the university
l'usine	(lₐ)	the factory

3. Drop the final **i** of the word **si** (*if*) before **il** (*he*) or **ils** (*they*).

Say:	**s'il vous plaît**	(sᵢ)	please
	S'il refusait?	(sᵢ)	What if he refused?
	s'ils voulaient y aller	(sᵢ)	if they wanted to go there
	s'ils étaient en France	(sᵢ)	if they were in France

4. Drop the final **oi** of **moi** (*me, myself*) and **toi** (*you, yourself*) when they come before the pronoun **en** (*of it, of them*).

Say:	**Donnez-m'en**	(mₒᵢ)	Give me some of it (them).
	Achète-t'en.	(tₒᵢ)	Buy yourself some of it (them).

5. And finally, drop the final **e** of the following common words before words beginning with vowels.

Say:	**lorsque**	**lorsqu'ils**	when they
	puisque	**puisqu'il**	since he
	quelque	**quelqu'un**	someone
	jusque	**jusqu'ici**	until now
	quoique	**quoiqu'il soit malade**	although he's ill

Note: Prohibited Elision

Elision does not take place

Before a number of words—often of Germanic origin—that begin with **h:**

Examples:

la hauteur	the height
le héros	the hero
le hors-d'œuvre	the appetizer
la hutte	the hut
la hache	the ax

Before **oui** (*yes*), **huit** (*eight*), or **onze** (*eleven*)

Unit 9 _____

Special Orthographic Features

Besides the accent marks that you studied in Unit 1, you must be familiar with four other orthographic signs in order to read French aloud. These are the **cedilla,** the **dieresis,** the **apostrophe,** and the **hyphen.**

The Cedilla

Used only under the letter **c** before **a, o,** or **u,** the **cedilla (ç)** alerts you to pronounce **c** like the *s* of English *sing.*

Say:		
	avançons	let's move forward
	façon	fashion, manner
	française	French girl or woman
	garçon	boy, waiter
	leçon	lesson
	je reçois	I receive
	soupçonner	to suspect

The Dieresis

This sign placed over a vowel shows you that it is pronounced as a syllable separate from the preceding vowel.

Say:		
	aigüe	high-pitched
	Noël	Christmas
	égoïsme	selfishness
	héroïque	heroic
	naïve	naive
	naïvement	naively

The Apostrophe

This sign indicates omission of a vowel sound. Vowel sounds are omitted in French when certain one-syllable words come before words that begin with a vowel sound.*

Say:			
l'amie	(la)	the friend (fem.)	
l'architecture	(la)	architecture	
l'édifice	(le)	the building	
l'escalier	(le)	the stairway	
l'heure	(la)	the hour	
l'hiver	(le)	winter	
s'il vous plaît	(si)	please	
J'ai de l'argent.	(Je—le)	I have some money.	
quelqu'un	(quelque)	somebody	

The Hyphen

In French, the hyphen connects certain closely related words in questions, commands, spelled numbers, and compound words.

Say:	
Comment vas-tu?	How are you?
Par où est-ce?	Which way is it?
Amusez-vous!	Have a good time!
Levez-vous!	Get up!
soixante-dix	seventy
quatre-vingt-deux	eighty-two
arc-en-ciel	rainbow
États-Unis	United States

---

* See also **Elision**, Unit 8.

Unit 10_____

Intonation

Intonation refers to the rise and fall of the voice, that is, its tone or pitch. Controlling your intonation when you speak French is important, because altering your tone can change the meaning of a sentence. In this unit you will practice the intonation patterns of statements, information questions, and yes / no questions.

Besides helping you master the intonation patterns, this practice will also draw together—in sentences—all the other pronunciation features you have studied up to this point.

Intonation in Statements

When you make a **statement** in French, end it with falling intonation.

Say: **Je vous remercie.**
Thank you.

Il est ici.
He's here.

Voilà l'hôtel.
There's the hotel.

Elles ne comprennent rien.
They don't understand at all.

On parle français en Suisse.
French is spoken in Switzerland.

Je suis américain.
I'm (an) American.

Je sais que vous êtes né en 1968.
I know that you were born in 1968.

Il arrivera lundi prochain.
He'll arrive next Monday.

Cette robe me plaît beaucoup.
I like this dress a lot.

Ils n'ont pas d'argent.
They don't have any money.

Les élèves entrent dans la salle de classe.
The students enter the classroom.

Les vacances vont commencer dans quelques jours.
Vacation is going to begin in a few days.

L'hiver est la plus froide des quatre saisons de l'année.
Winter is the coldest of the four seasons of the year.

Information Questions

An **information question** begins with a question word and requires an answer that provides information beyond just **oui** or **non**. Just as in English, French information questions end with a falling tone. As you practice the following information questions, note the question words with which they begin.

Say: **Combien de sœurs avez-vous?**
How many sisters do you have?

Combien de temps m'avez-vous attendu?
How long did you wait for me?

Comment vas-tu?
How are you?

Comment allez-vous?
How are you?

Lequel préférez-vous?
Which do you prefer?

Laquelle de ces robes veux-tu porter?
Which of these dresses do you want to take?

Où es-tu allée ce soir?
Where did you go tonight?

Où est-ce que Michelle habite?
Where does Michelle live?

Pourquoi êtes-vous ici?
Why are you here?

Pourquoi ne m'avez-vous pas téléphoné?
Why haven't you phoned me?

Quand l'avion va-t-il atterrir à Paris?
When is the airplane going to land in Paris?

Quand est-ce que le train va arriver?
When is the train going to arrive?

Que voulez-vous?
What do you want?

Qu'est-ce que les garçons ont fait hier?
What did the boys do yesterday?

Quel âge avez-vous?
How old are you?

Quels sont vos livres préférés?
What are your favorite books?

À quelle heure arrive le train?
What time does the train arrive?

Quelles sont les villes principales de la France?
What are the main cities of France?

Qui est là?
Who's there?

Qui est-ce que tu regardes?
Whom are you looking at?

À quoi pensez-vous?
What are you thinking about?

Qu'est-ce qui la rend heureuse?
What is she happy about?

Yes/no Questions

These questions, which can be answered with a simple **oui** or **non,** end with rising intonation. The rising tone expresses uncertainty; you really do not know whether the answer to your question will be **oui** or **non.**

Say: **Tu vas à l'école?**
Are you going to school?

Tu me comprends?
Do you understand me?

Parlez-vous français?
Do you speak French?

Aimez-vous cet acteur?
Do you like that actor?

Voulez-vous aller au cinéma?
Do you want to go to the movies?

Avez-vous un crayon?
Do you have a pencil?

Cherchez-vous les livres?
Are you looking for the books?

Il est très sympathique, n'est-ce pas?
He's very nice, isn't he?

Vous êtes d'accord, n'est-ce pas?
You do agree, don't you?

Est-il ici?
Is he here?

Est-ce qu'il est ici?
Is he here?

Est-ce que tu as déjà dîné?
Have you already had dinner?

Est-ce que vous connaissez mon ami?
Do you know my friend?

Est-ce que vous parlez français?
Do you speak French?

Vous parlez français?
Do you speak French?

Part Three
Appendix

The French Alphabet in Sequence

LETTER	NAME	KEY WORD(S)	PAGE
a	a	madame	1
		passe (open)	1
b	bé	beau	16
c	cé	calme (= k)	20
		cent, cinq (= s)	20
		ça (with cedilla)	20
d	dé	danger	16
e	e	bébé (closed)	2
		très (open)	3
		me (mute)	3
		facile (silent)	4
f	effe	chef	17
g	gé	guerre (before **a, o,**	
		u or consonant)	22
		général (before **e, i**)	22
h	ache	homme	17
i	i	difficile	4
		spécial (semivowel)	5
j	ji	jambe	22
k	ka	kilomètre	16
l	elle	langue	23
		famille (= y)	24
m	emme	mardi	16
n	enne	noir	16
o	o	potage (open)	5
		nôtre (closed)	5
p	pé	papa	19

q	ku	question	21
r	erre	rouge	24
s	esse	suspect (= s)	17
		chose (= z)	18
t	té	table	19
		nation (= s)	19
u	u	lune	6
v	vé	vache	16
w	double vé	wagon	18
x	iks	excellence (= ks)	26
		examen (= gs)	26
y	i grec	Yves	5
		yeux	24
z	zède	zone	16

Vowel Combinations

VOWEL	KEY WORD(S)	PAGE
ai	lait (open)	12
	je parlerai (closed)	12
au, eau	gauche, bateau	12
ei	neige	13
eu, œu	heure, cœur (open)	13
	bleu (closed)	13
oi	moi	14
ou	amour (= u)	14
	oui (= w)	15
ui	huit	15

Consonant Combinations

COMBINATION	KEY WORD(S)	PAGE
ch	cheval	27
	chrome (= k)	27
gn	espagnol	28
ph	photo	28
th	thé	28